Basics

wrapped loops

1 Make sure you have no less than 1¼ in. (32mm) of wire above your bead. With the tip of your chainnose pliers, grasp the wire directly above the bead. Bend the wire (above the pliers) into a right angle.
2 Using roundnose pliers, position the jaws vertically in the bend.

3 Bring the wire over the top jaw of the roundnose pliers.
4 Keep the jaws vertical and reposition the pliers so the lower jaw fits snugly in the loop. Curve the wire downward around the bottom of the roundnose pliers. This is the first half of a wrapped loop.

5 Position the jaws of your chainnose pliers across the loop.
6 Wrap the wire around the wire stem, covering the stem between the loop and the top bead. Trim the excess wire and gently press the cut end close to the wraps with chainnose pliers.

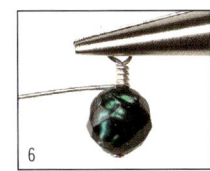

loops: opening and closing

1 Hold the jump ring with two pairs of chainnose pliers or chainnose and roundnose pliers, as shown.

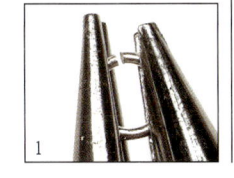

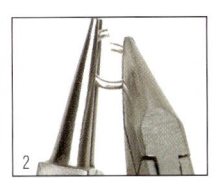

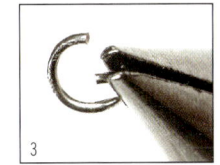

2 To open the jump ring, bring one pair of pliers toward you and push the other away.
3 The open jump ring. Reverse the steps to close the ring.

loops: plain

1 Trim the wire or head pin ⅜ in. (10mm) above the top bead. Make a right angle-bend close to the bead.
2 Grab the wire's tip with roundnose pliers. Roll the wire to form a half circle. Release the wire.

3 Position the pliers in the loop again and continue rolling, forming a centered circle above the bead.
4 The finished loop.

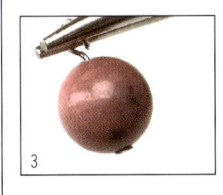

flattened crimp

1 Hold the crimp using the tip of your chainnose pliers. Squeeze the pliers firmly to flatten the crimp. Tug the clasp to make sure the crimp has a solid grip on the wire. If the wire slides, repeat the steps with a new crimp.
2 The flattened crimp.

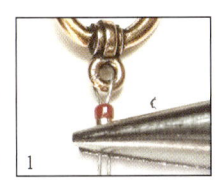

folded crimp

1 Position the crimp in the notch closest to the crimping pliers' handle.
2 Separate the wires and firmly squeeze the crimp.

3 Move the crimp into the notch at the pliers' tip and hold the crimp as shown. Squeeze the crimp, folding it in half at the indentation.
4 The folded crimp.

square knot

1 Cross the left-hand cord over the right-hand cord, and then bring it under the right-hand cord from back to front. Pull it up in front so both ends are facing upwards.
2 Cross right over left, forming a loop, and go through the loop, again from back to front. Pull the ends to tighten the knot.

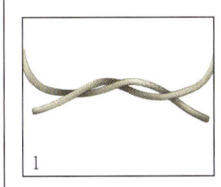

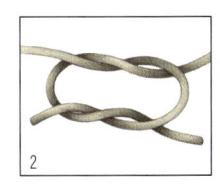

Easy wire earrings

You don't have to purchase findings every time you make a pair of earrings. You can make your own with wire or, as in these luscious examples, string a long piece of wire with beads and shape the unbeaded portion to hook through your ear. The most important thing to remember is to file smooth the end of the wire that passes through your ear to prevent scratching or cutting your earlobes. Also, make sure to choose beads with holes large enough for 20-gauge or thicker wire.

The basic earring is the simple cherry quartz style (above right). The other two earrings are variations on the basic theme. Each makes use of a second length of wire that wraps around the wire between the main beads.

For all these designs, start with a small spiral at one end of the wire to hold the beads on. Then string the beads and shape the wire. You can bend the wire at the back in any direction to position the earrings as desired alongside your face. Remember to make the two dangles mirror images of each other.

cherry quartz earrings (above, right)

❶ Cut the wire into two 5-in. (12.7cm) lengths. Use the tip of a roundnose pliers to form a small loop (see "Basics," p. 3 and **photo a**). Hold the loop in a chain-nose pliers and, using your fingers, press the wire around the loop for ½ revolution (**photo b**).

❷ String an oblong bead, a spacer, an oblong bead, and another spacer. Above the last bead, curve the wire into a 180-degree turn that's about the width of your ring finger with a tail the length of your pinkie. The wire tail should curve close to the beads, extend a bit below them, and then curve away toward the back to form a hook. Shape the hook so the spiral at the bottom faces forward (**photo c**).

❸ Cut off the excess wire with the flat side of the wire cutters against the earring end (**photo d**). Then file the cut smooth and round the end slightly. Make the second earring to match.

carnelian earrings (above, left)

❶ Cut the wire into two 5-in. lengths and two 4-in. (10cm) lengths. Make a tiny loop at the bottom of one long wire for the earring bottom. Repeat with a short wire and bend this loop at a right angle to the wire (**photo e**). String this loop onto the long wire.

❷ String the largest flat bead on the long wire and bend the short wire flat

tip

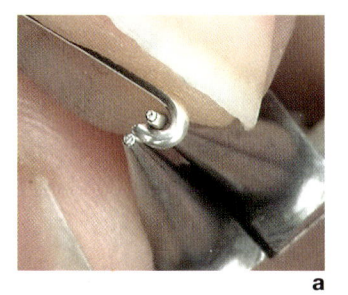

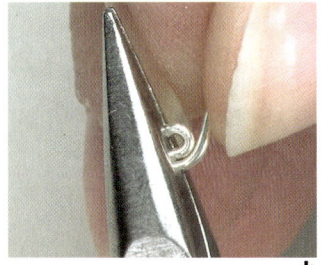

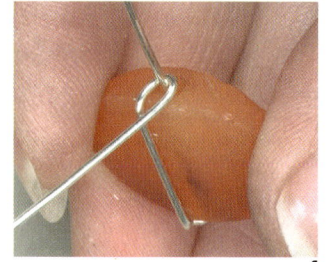

great surface for beads

A material that's wonderful to bead on is Velux, a synthetic fabric often used for blankets. You can cut the material to fit a tray or any other working surface. It's machine washable, and the nap keeps beads from rolling around. Inexpensive twin-size Velux blankets are available at discount stores. Buy one and cut it into pads for yourself and your beading friends. – *Amy Bradley*

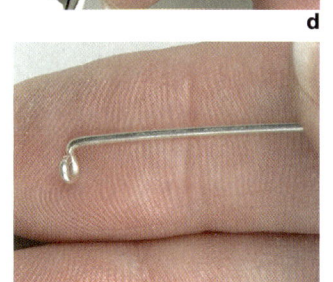

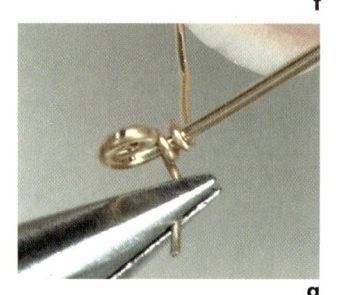

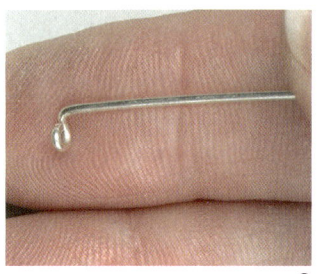

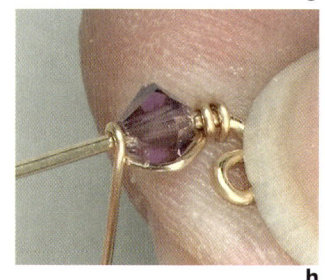

against its back. Wrap once around the long wire above the bead (**photo f**). Repeat with the medium bead and the small bead. End the short wire by wrapping it twice above the small bead and cutting the tail flush. Pinch it in place with chainnose pliers.

❸ Shape the top as in the "cherry quartz earring." Make the second earring to match the first.

crystal-embellished jade earrings (opposite, middle)

❶ Make a small loop at the end of a 4½-in. (11.4cm) length of 20-gauge wire and spiral the wire ¼ turn around the loop so the loop curves upward like a Turkish slipper.

❷ Grip the tail end of a 5-in. length of 24-gauge wire with chainnose pliers and wrap it twice around the 20-gauge wire just above the upward-curving loop (**photo g**). String one crystal onto the earring wire and, with your fingers, wrap the thin wire once above the crystal, locking the crystal in place (**photo h**).

❸ String a stone bead on the earring wire and three crystals on the thin wire. Bring bare wire up under the stone bead so the crystals hug the side of the bead. Wrap tightly twice above the stone (**photo i**). Repeat this step twice. End the thin wire with three tight wraps above the third stone. Stack the crystal curves in a straight line or offset them with slightly less than two wraps each.

❹ Shape the top and shaft as in the "cherry quartz earring." Make the second earring to match. ◌

– *Louise Malcolm*

materials

cherry quartz earrings
- 10 in. (25cm) 20-gauge sterling silver wire, half-hard
- **4** 4-5mm flat silver spacers
- **4** 16 x 12mm oblong stone or glass beads

carnelian earrings
- 18 in. (46cm) 20-gauge sterling silver wire, half-hard
- **6** graduated flat, oval beads (the ones pictured are from Afghan Tribal Arts, 847-602-6651)

jade and crystal earrings
- 9 in. (23cm) 20-gauge gold-filled wire, half-hard
- **6** 7 x 10mm faceted stone beads
- **20** 4mm bicone crystals
- 10 in. 24-gauge gold-filled wire, dead soft

Tools: roundnose and chainnose pliers, wire cutters, jeweler's file

Furnace glass earrings

Furnace glass, with its vibrant colors and alluring depth, is beautiful, but can be a challenge to use as it usually has either very large or nonexistent holes. The designs on these pages show two creative approaches for making earrings with furnace glass.

For the earrings opposite above, use tigertail wire strung with seed beads to dangle the unusual triangular furnace pieces. Then, connect this element to a wire head pin that is strung with more furnace glass or other assorted beads.

❶ String about 6 in. (15cm) of seed beads on a 12-14 in. (31-36cm) length of .012 tigertail. Wrap the wire covered with seed beads closely and snugly several times around the triangular bead. Push the seed beads together so no wire shows. Remove excess beads and bring the wire ends together through a crimp bead. Feed the ends back through the crimp to make a small loop. Crimp the crimp bead (see "Basics," p. 3). Hang the wrapped bead from the loop on the wire head pin (**photo a**).
❷ String a furnace bead, a metal spacer, another furnace bead, and another spacer on the head pin. Using a furnace glass bead with a large hole will conceal the loops and the crimp and still allow the wrapped bead to dangle freely.
❸ Make a loop at the top of the head pin (see "Basics") and attach it to the earring finding. Make the other earring to match. ◐ – *Alice Korach*

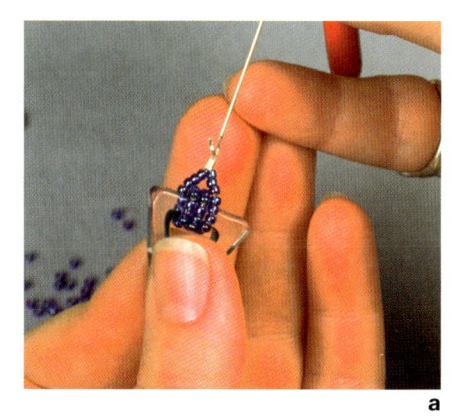

materials
- 2 large furnace glass triangles
- 4 small (7-10mm) furnace glass slices
- 4 metal spacer beads
- seed beads
- 2 crimp beads
- 12-14 in. (31-36cm) .012 tigertail wire
- 2 head pins
- pair earring wires with loop

Tools: roundnose and chainnose pliers, diagonal wire cutters

For the earrings shown opposite below, string three pieces of furnace glass on a wire triangle that hangs from a jump ring, and then dangle the jump ring from an earring finding. The key to this design is to make sure your wire side pieces are the same length and that all your loops are exactly the same size. You may want to put a pencil mark on the jaws of your roundnose pliers to ensure equal loops. The furnace glass slices should fit over the loops; if they don't, thread them onto the wire crossbar before making the second wire loop.

❶ For each earring, cut three ⅞-in. (2.2cm) pieces of wire. Make a loop at both ends of each piece of wire (see "Basics," p. 3) for a total of six loops.
❷ Use two pairs of pliers to adjust the position of the loops (**photo b**). On the two side wires, the loops should be at 90-degree angles to each other. On the horizontal wire, make sure they are in exactly the same plane.
❸ To connect the three pieces of wire into a triangle, open a loop on one side wire by bending it out of the plane of the loop (see "Basics") and hook one loop of the horizontal bar to it. Close the loop by bending the end back into the plane. Slide three furnace glass beads—small, large, small—onto the bar. Attach the other side wire to the bar.
❹ Attach the side wires to a jump ring with the loops sitting parallel (**photo c**). Open the loop on the earring finding and hook the jump ring to it. Close the loop. Make the other earring to match. ◐
– *Gloria Harris*

materials
- 2 large (15–20mm) furnace glass slices
- 4 small (7–10mm) furnace glass slices
- 12 in. (30cm) 20-gauge wire or 6 head pins
- 2 5mm jump rings
- pair earring wires with loops

Tools: roundnose and chainnose pliers, diagonal wire cutters

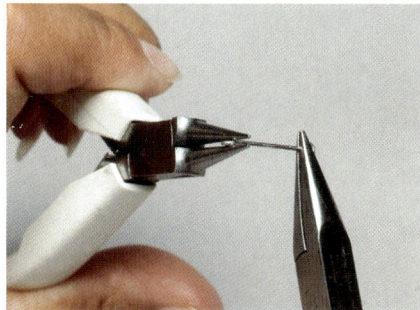

Tornado twist earrings

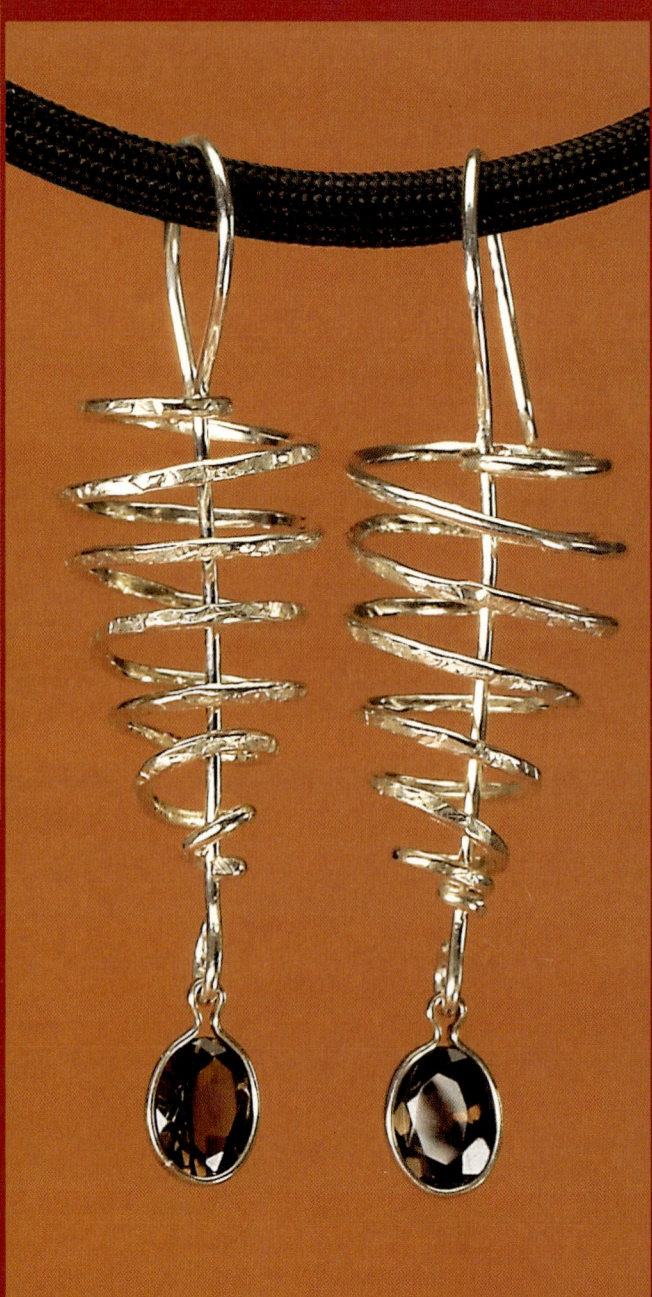

Create the swirling funnel shape of these earrings freehand using roundnose pliers or on the conical end of an anvil. Whether you see spirals or tornados, you'll be blown away by these quick and easy, lightweight wire earrings.

The earwire inside the spiral may be left plain or embellished. String the center wire with 2mm silver or seed beads or try wrapping it with 24-gauge twist wire. Blacken one of the twist wires with liver of sulfur solution to make it stand out from the other one.

twist wire spirals

❶ Cut a 2½-in. (6cm) piece of 20-gauge round wire. Refer to the **template** below and use a pen or pencil to form a hook for the earwire (**photo a**).

❷ Make a slight bend on the short wire below the hook (**template**) and file the end smooth. This end of the wire will be going in your earlobe, so make sure it doesn't have a jagged end.

❸ Cut the twist wire in half, so you have two 10-in. (25.4cm) lengths. Form a funnel-shaped spiral with one of the wires using roundnose pliers, or wrap the wire around the conical end of an anvil (**photo b**).

❹ Start at the large end of the spiral and make a small loop at the end of the wire, but don't close it (see "Basics," p. 3 and **photo c**). Center the loop above the first coil using chainnose pliers (**photo d**). Repeat at the other end of the spiral. This spiral has seven coils. If you make a smaller spiral, you may need to trim the wire before making the second loop.

❺ To add a wire wrap to the earring, cut a 5-in. (13cm) piece of 24-gauge twist wire and wrap it around the straight part of the earwire for approximately one inch (2.5cm) (**photo e**). Trim the excess twist wire.

❻ Position the earwire in the center of the spiral and through the loops. Use chainnose pliers to squeeze the loops closed around the earwire (**photo f**). If you added a wire wrap to the earwire, you might have to open the loops slightly. Attach the loops above and below the wrapped wire (**photo g**).

❼ Make a loop at the end of the earwire.

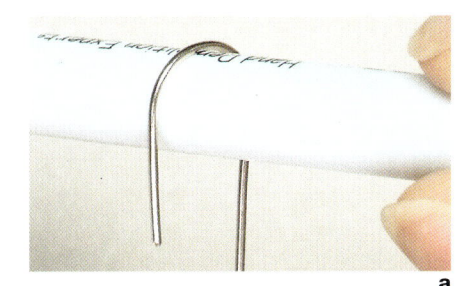

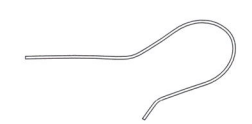

❽ String a 6 or 8mm bead and a bead cap on a head pin and make a loop above the bead cap. Open the loop sideways (see "Basics") and attach it to the loop at the bottom of the earwire (**photo h**). Close the loop tightly.

❾ Make a second earring the mirror image of the first so the spirals turn in opposite directions.

textured wire spirals

❶ Form the earwire with a 2½-in. piece of 20-gauge wire as in the previous earring (steps 1 and 2).

❷ Cut a 10-in. piece of 20-gauge wire and hammer it to add texture. Form the wire into a funnel-shaped spiral as described in step 3 of "twist wire spirals" (**photo b**).

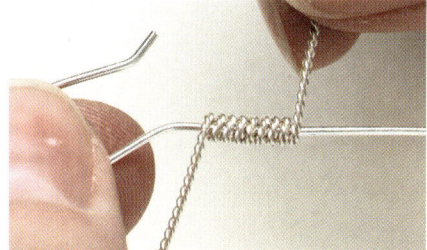

❸ Follow steps 4–9 for the "twist wire spirals." ○ – *Wendy Witchner*

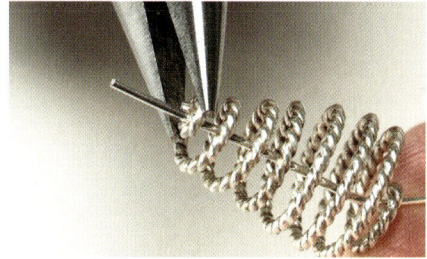

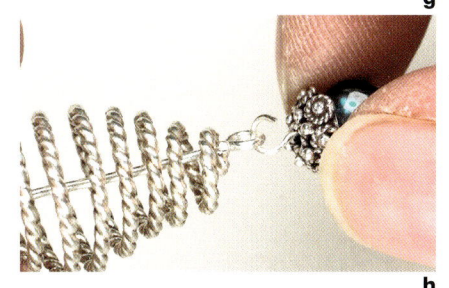

materials
- 5 in. (13cm) 20-gauge sterling silver wire
- 20 in. (51cm) 20-gauge sterling silver wire, twist or round
- 2 6-8mm pearls or glass beads
- 2 bead caps
- 2 head pins

Tools: roundnose and chainnose pliers, wire cutters, metal file

Optional: 10 in. (25cm) 24-gauge twisted sterling silver wire, anvil and hammer, liver of sulfur or other oxidizing solution

Stone flowers

For the modest investment of wire, semi-precious stones, and a few beads, you can make a pair of dazzling stone flower earrings like these. The large rose quartz earrings above use beads with holes through the long axis. The smaller scapolite earrings, above right, are made with briolette-style beads with holes through the tip.

rose quartz earrings

❶ Slip a 6-in. (15cm) length of 20-gauge wire through a flat gold-tone bead, leaving ¾ in. (2cm) extended from one side. Bend the short wire end against the side and flat across the back of the bead. At the center of the bead, bend the wire at a right angle to project straight up for the earring post (**photo a**).
❷ Bend the long end across the bead and wrap once around the base of the post. Then spiral the wire once around the bead about ⅛ in. (3mm) beyond the edge (**photo b**) and trim.
❸ Cut a 14-in. (36cm) length of the 24-gauge wire and center it in the hole of the center bead with the ends above the wire spiral.
❹ On each end, string a rose quartz bead and a seed bead. Bend the wire to the back of the rose quartz bead with chainnose pliers, keeping the seed bead at the tip of the quartz bead. Be careful not to pinch it with the pliers or it will break (**photo c**).
❺ Wrap each wire 1¼ times around the post and bring each out above the spiral next to the first petals. Repeat steps 4 and 5 to make six petals.
❻ Bring the wire tails back to the post, going under the spiral, and wrap both around the post 2 or 3 times (**photo d**).

❼ Cut the posts to the desired length and file a slight notch near the end on each to catch the ear nut. File the end of each post smooth.

scapolite earrings

❶ Thread six scapolite briolettes on an ultra-fine head pin (a fine head pin is too thick for these beads) and twist the ends of the pin into a circle with about ¹⁄₁₆ in. (1.6mm) of ease (**photo e**).
❷ Fold a 6-in. length of 20-gauge wire in half and bend the fold into a tight hook with the tip of a chainnose pliers. Holding the hook flat in the pliers, spiral the doubled wire around the hook. Keep regrasping the completed portion of the spiral in the pliers to make a tight, round wrap (**photo f**). When the spiral is about ⅜ in. (1cm) across, stop wrapping the outer wire,

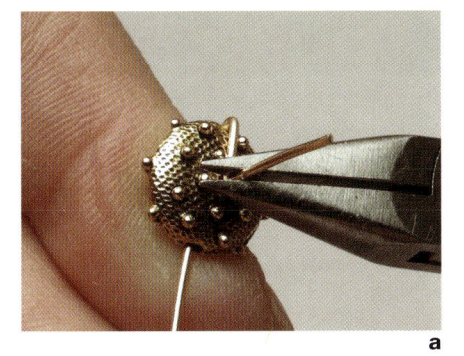

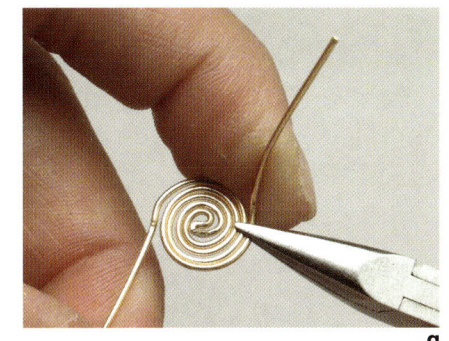

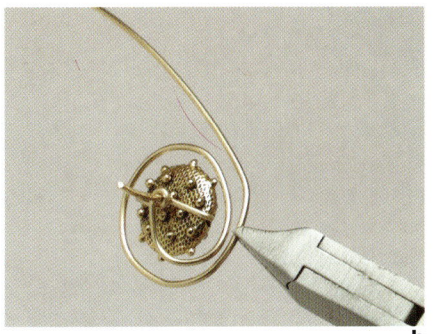

but continue wrapping the inner wire until the wires are opposite each other (**photo g**).

❸ Bend both wires to extend perpendicular to the spiral and place the spiral face down on a table. Set the circle of beads face down over the spiral with the wires between opposite beads and outside the head pin circle. One wire should be one bead away from the head pin join.

❹ Wrap one end of the head pin around each wire (**photo h**). Then bend the wires so they cross behind the spiral and parallel to it.

❺ Where they meet at the center, bend one wire perpendicular to the spiral for the earring post. Wrap the other wire around the base of the post 1-2 times (**photo i**). Finish as in step 7 above. ●
– Gloria Harris

materials

rose quartz earrings
- **12** 12 x 9mm flat oval rose quartz beads
- **2** 10mm gold-tone pewter flat, round beads
- **12 in. (30cm)** 20-gauge gold-filled wire, half-hard
- **28 in. (71cm)** 24-gauge gold-filled wire, half-hard
- **12** size 11º gold seed beads
- pair earring nuts

scapolite earrings
- **12** 8 x 6mm faceted scapolite or other briolettes (artgemsinc.com)
- **2** ultra-fine-gauge gold-tone head pins
- **12 in.** 20-gauge gold-filled wire, half-hard
- pair earring nuts

Tools: roundnose and chainnose pliers, wire cutters, jeweler's file

tip

safe wire cutting

Working with wire is fun and rewarding. The excess pieces that you trim off can be unpredictable and hazardous, however. To prevent possible eye injury, always press a spare finger against the end of the wire that you are cutting. This will ensure that the wire drops down onto your work surface.
– Sarah Evans

Spacer bar earrings

If you want to make eye-catching earrings, sometimes the best place to start is with a finding that's meant for something else. In these two examples, spacer bars that are intended for a necklace or bracelet provide great starting points for delightful dangles.

The twinkling crystal earrings at left look like tiny waterfalls. They shimmer with every move. Link the crystals together with wrapped loops for lots of movement.

Head pins with ball ends were used for this project. If you use regular head pins, you may need to string a size 15º seed bead before you pass through the spacer bar. When making the wrapped loops, work close to the tip of your roundnose pliers so that your loops are small. If you use crystals in several different colors, vary the placement of the colors so the mix is distributed over the dangles.

prepare the spacer bar

1 Pass a head pin through the first hole of the spacer bar and then string a crystal on the head pin. Turn a small (2mm diameter) wrapped loop (see "Basics," p. 3) below the crystal (**photo a**).

2 Repeat step 1 for each hole on the spacer bar except the central one.

For the silver and pearl earrings at left, make the three dangles for each earring first, attaching each to a length of chain. Then attach the chain sections to the head pins that go through the spacer bar. Because the beads are small and the chain is fine, connect all parts with small wrapped loops.

1 To make the two end dangles, begin by stringing a flat pearl onto each of two head pins, curved side first. String a silver spacer and then another flat pearl, flat side first. Begin a small wrapped loop, but before completing the wrap, attach a three-link length of chain (see "Basics," p. 3 and **photo e**).

2 For the center dangle, string a large pearl on a head pin and top it with a silver spacer. Begin a small wrapped loop and pull a four-link length of chain into the loop before completing the wrap.

❸ Cut a 3-in. (8cm) length of 24-gauge wire. Make a small wrapped loop on one end. Pass the wire through the central hole on the spacer bar and string a crystal. Turn a wrapped loop below the crystal (**photo b**).

make the components

❶ Make five crystal and head pin units by stringing a crystal on a head pin and making a wrapped loop above the crystal.
❷ Make 15 crystal and wire units by cutting a 2½-in. (6cm) length of wire, starting a wrapped loop, and stringing a crystal on each. Start a wrapped loop on the other side of each crystal.

make and connect the dangles

❶ Make two chains containing two wire units and one head pin unit. Complete the wraps after connecting the loops. Link the top unfinished loop of one chain to the loop below the first spacer bar hole and finish the wrap (**photo c**). Link the other below the fifth spacer bar hole.
❷ Make two chains containing three wire units and one head-pin unit. Complete the wraps on the connected loops. Link the top loop of one chain to the loop below the second spacer-bar hole and the other chain to the loop below the fourth spacer bar hole.
❸ Make a chain containing four wire units and one head-pin unit. Link it to the loop below the third or central hole on the spacer bar.
❹ Use the remaining wire unit to connect the loop on the earring finding to the loop above the central hole on the spacer bar (**photo d**).
❺ Make the other earring to match. ●
– Pam O'Connor

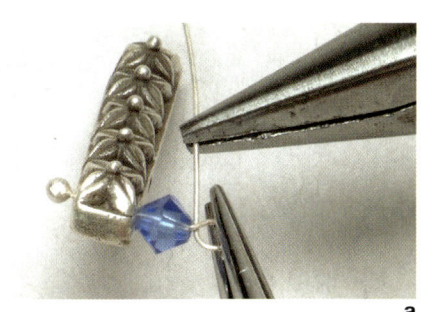

materials

- **2** 5-hole spacer bars
- pair earring findings with loops
- **50** 4mm bicone crystals
- **18** head pins with ball ends
- **7 ft.** 24-gauge sterling silver wire

Tools: roundnose and chainnose pliers, wire cutters

---

❸ For the two end holes on the spacer bar, string a flat pearl curved side first on a head pin, and then a spacer. Go through an end hole and string a spacer, then a flat pearl, flat side first. Begin a small wrapped loop and pull the end of a three-link chain dangle into the loop before completing the wrap (**photo f**).
❹ Use a scrap piece of head-pin wire to attach the center dangle. Begin with a small wrapped loop and pull the end of the four-link chain dangle into it before wrapping. String a flat pearl curved side first, then a spacer, and go through the center hole of the bar from bottom to top. String a spacer, then a flat pearl flat side first (**photo g**). End with a small wrapped loop and attach the earring finding before completing the wrap.
❺ Make the other earring to match. ●
– Louise Malcolm

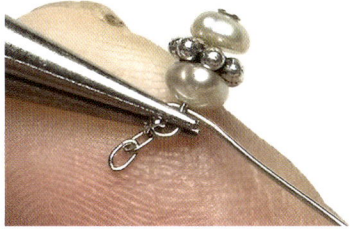

materials

- **1½ in.** (3.8cm) 2.2mm silver cable chain
- **10-12** ultra-fine gauge head pins
- **20** 1.5 x 3.5mm flat pearls, small crystals, or rondelles
- **18** 1 x 4mm silver spacers
- **2** 8 x 6mm pearls or crystals
- pair earring wires with loops

Tools: roundnose and chainnose pliers, wire cutters

Spiral earrings

Wire coils and spirals have been used in jewelry throughout the ages, as is evident in Daniela Mascetti and Amanda Triossi's book, *Earrings, From Antiquity to the Present*. These earrings feature overlapping spirals similar to those found in pre-Columbian jewelry.

Form the components, assemble the pieces, and adjust as needed. Practicing on some inexpensive craft wire is a good idea if you haven't made spirals before.

getting started
❶ Cut the wire into two 3-in. (7.6cm), 5-in. (12.9cm), 7-in. (18cm), and 9-in. (23cm) pieces. Cut the remaining wire into six 1-in. (2.5cm) pieces.
❷ Make six S-links from the 1-in. wires. These connect the spirals, so the loops should be a uniform ¼ in. (6mm) each. Make a loop at one end using roundnose pliers. Make a loop at the other end facing the opposite direction (**photo a**). If you trim the excess wire and the wire cutters leave chiseled points as shown in the photo, it's best to file the ends so the wire is flush against itself. This forms a more secure connection.

making the spirals
❶ Bend one 9-in. wire in half (at the 4½-in./11.5cm mark) and wrap it around the roundnose pliers so a loop is formed in the middle. Make a small loop on each end (**photo b**).
❷ Begin the spiral by rolling each end loop in on itself using chainnose pliers (**photo c**). If you put painter's (blue masking) tape on your pliers, you won't leave marks on the wire and you won't leave sticky residue on your pliers. Grip the loop in the pliers, push the length of the wire around it, and roll it into a flat spiral. Continuously reposition the pliers to keep the spiral flat and tight. Continue until there is about ¼ in. between the center loop and the spiral center. Repeat with the other half of the wire as shown in **photo d**.
❸ Place roundnose pliers between the center loop and the spiral. Bend the spiral down around the pliers (**photo e**). Repeat with the other side and adjust the spirals as needed (**photo f**).
❹ Make similar spirals with the remaining wires.

making the dangles
Make the dangles by stringing a small silver bead and a stone bead on a head pin. Attach the dangles to the bottom spiral unit with either a plain or wrapped loop.
❶ String a 3mm silver bead and a stone drop bead on a head pin and

tip

even drops

To make your drops identical, put one bead on a head pin and, leaving room for a loop, trim the extra wire. Use the excess bit as a guide for cutting the other pin.
– Maureen Murray

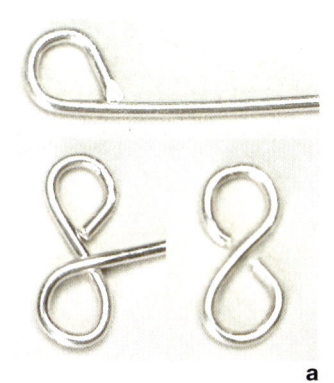

a

materials
- 4½ ft. (1.2m) 22-gauge sterling silver wire, dead soft
- 4 in. (10cm) 22-gauge sterling silver wire, half-hard for earwires or **1** pair sterling earring findings with loops
- **2** ½-in. (1.3cm) stone or glass drops
- **2** 3mm silver bead or small daisy spacers
- **2** head pins

Tools: roundnose and chainnose pliers, wire cutter, ruler, jeweler's file or sandpaper

earwires

Attach an earwire to the loop between the large spirals. The front of the finding should face the same direction as the front of the spirals. You can make an earwire by taking a 2-in. (5cm) length of wire and making a plain or over-rolled loop connected to the center loop of the largest spiral pair. (Half-hard wire is best for findings as it holds its shape better, but if you use half-hard wire for the spirals, they won't be as easy to bend.) Bend the wire up as if you were going to coil it around the loop, but instead wrap it in the other direction with roundnose pliers to form the hook (**photo i**). Put a slight curve at the end of the earwire and trim to the desired length. You should smooth the end with a needle file. If you don't have a file, rub the end of the wire on a piece of fine-grit sandpaper. Earwires must be free of sandpaper residue before you wear them. A little rubbing alcohol or soap and water will do the trick. – *Kelli Peduzzi*

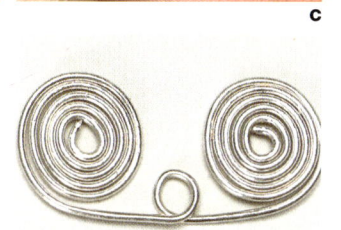

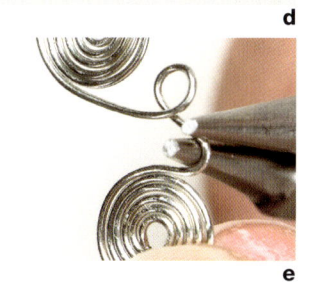

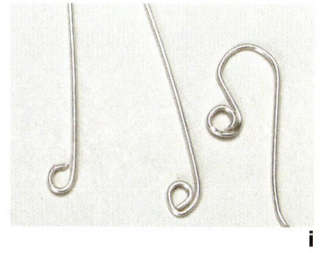

make a small loop at the top. If you are using a heavy bead, allow some extra wire for a wrapped loop (see "Basics," p.3).

❷ Attach the dangle to the smallest spiral as shown in **photo g**, or use a wrapped loop as in **photo h**. This makes a great earring all by itself!

putting it together

Connect the spirals with the S-links, working from largest to smallest by twisting the link loops opened and closed (see "Basics").

❶ Open the loop of an S-link and slip it through the center loop of the largest spiral, then close the loop.

❷ Open the other loop of the same S-link and slip it through the center loop of the next size spiral and close. The largest spirals should overlap the next set and so on down the line.

❸ Connect the remaining spirals, including the smallest component with the dangle, the same way.

❹ Use your fingers and chainnose pliers to even out the spirals, then make the other earring.

Bead & Button • Fun Beaded Earrings

Star-spangled stitches

Red, white, and blue designs are perennial favorites among many beaders, especially since the events of September 11, 2001. Demonstrate your patriotism as well as your passion for beads with these modified square-stitch star earrings.

making the points

1 Thread a needle with 1 yd. (.9m) of Nymo. String size 11º seed beads in the following pattern: one blue, one white, one blue, one white, two blue, one white, one blue, two red, ten white, two red, one blue, one white, and one blue. Slide the beads down to about 3 in. (7.6cm) from the thread's end. Tie the beads into a circle with a square knot (see "Basics," p. 3 and **figure 1**).

2 To begin the first point, pick up four blue beads and count over the first five beads strung (one blue, one white, one blue, one white, and one blue). Sew back through one blue, one white, and one blue, turn, and sew back through the last two blue beads added with this row (**figure 2**).

3 Pick up one blue, one white, and one blue. Sew back through the beads added in step 2 and the three beads just added.

4 Pick up two blue beads. Sew back through the three beads added in step 3 and the two beads just added (**figure 3**).

5 Pick up one blue bead and sew back through the two beads added in step 4.

6 To make the loop for hanging the star, sew through the blue bead added in step 5 and pick up six blue beads. Sew back through the step 5 blue bead again and through the loop once more for reinforcement, finally exiting the blue bead added in step 5 (**figure 4**).

7 Sew through the beads to exit the last bead of the point's first row (**figure 5**).

8 Following the bead pattern in **figure 6**, stitch points 2-5 of the star with the same thread path used to add the first point (steps 1-5 and 7).

completing the star

1 Exit the end blue bead in the fifth point's first row and pick up four blue beads. Sew through one blue, one white, and one blue bead at the end of the first point's first row and the last two blue beads added. Go through the only white bead on the second point's first row (**figure 7**).

16   Bead&Button • Fun Beaded Earrings

2 Pick up one blue, one white, and one blue bead. Sew though the last two blue beads added in step 1 and back through the white and second blue bead just added (**figure 8, a-b**).

3 Pick up one blue, one white, and one blue bead. Sew through the first two blue beads added in step 1, the three beads just added, and the second red bead in the fifth point's first row (**figure 8, b-c**).

4 Pick up three red beads. Sew back through the first blue and the white bead added in step 3 and back through the last two red beads added (**figure 9, a-b**).

5 Pick up three red beads and sew through the last blue and white beads in the row above, the last two red beads just added, and through the first two white beads on the third point's first row (**figure 9, b-c**).

6 Pick up three white beads and sew through the last two red beads added in step 4, last two white beads just added, and the first three white beads in the fourth point's first row (**figure 9 c-d**).

7 Sew through the beads to exit by the thread's tail end and tie the thread ends together in another square knot.

8 Glue the knot and sew the working end through a few rows before trimming the thread close to the beads. Thread a needle to the tail end and sew through a few rows before trimming the thread close to the beads.

9 Open the loop on the earring wire (see "Basics") and insert the loop at the top of the star's first point. Close the loop on the earring finding.

10 Make the other earring to match. ●
– Dragonfay.com

materials

- 4g each of 11º seed beads in red, white, and blue
- Nymo D beading thread, black
- beading needle, #12
- **2** earring wires
- G-S Hypo Cement

Tools: chainnose pliers

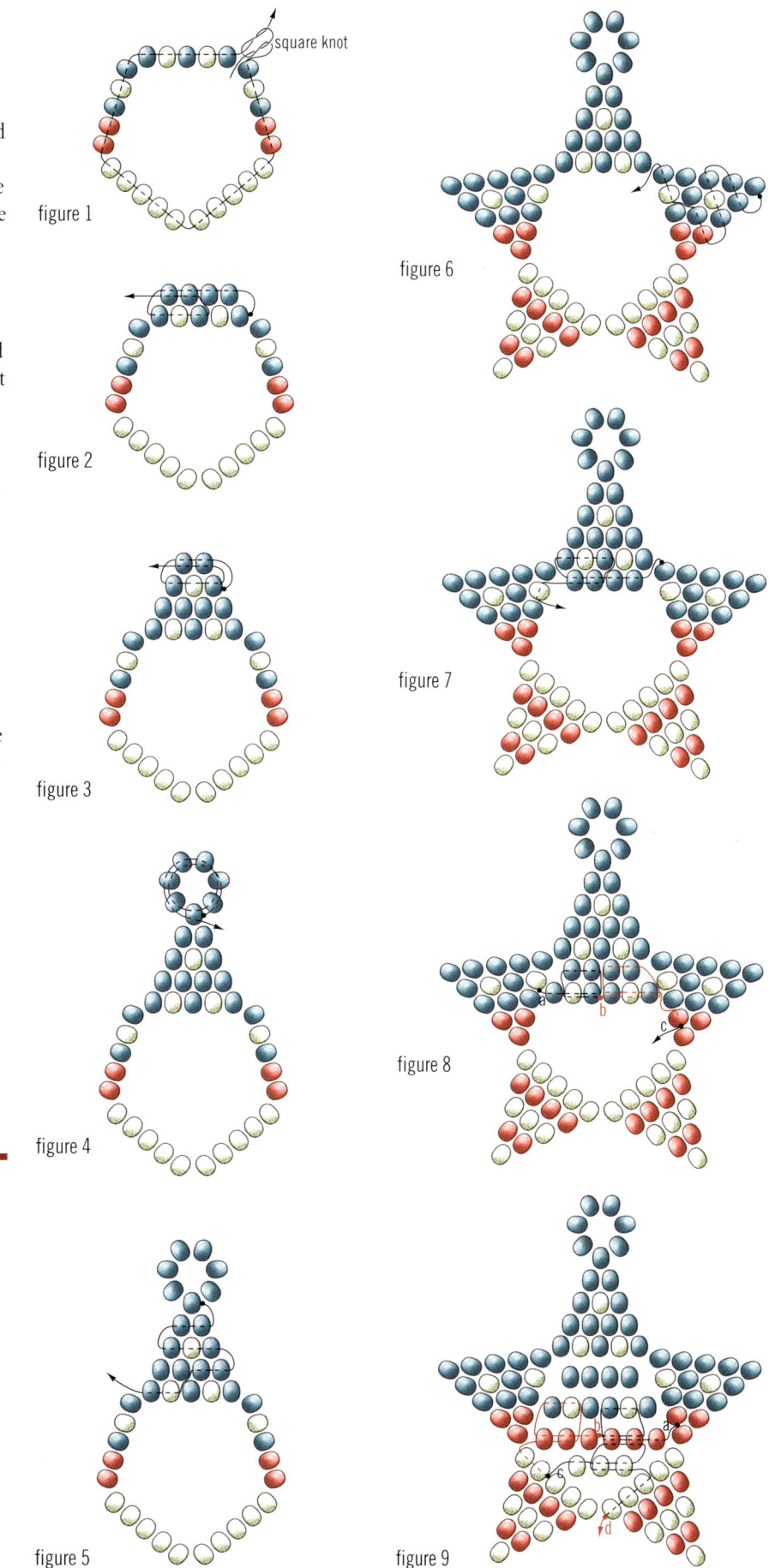

figure 1

figure 2

figure 3

figure 4

figure 5

figure 6

figure 7

figure 8

figure 9

Bead&Button • Fun Beaded Earrings   17

Free-form wire shapes

Free-form wire design is fun and has limitless possibilities. Use these earrings as a starting point for your own designs.

Use either 14- or 16-gauge wire. 16-gauge wire is easier to form since it isn't as thick as 14-gauge. The earrings will also be lighter, so you can add beaded dangles or wraps.

1 Cut the wire in half so you have two equal 16-in. (41cm) lengths. If the ends of the wire are sharp, round them with a metal file.

2 Grasp the end of one of the wires in the middle of the roundnose pliers. Bring the wire over one jaw of the pliers to form a loop (**photo a**). This is the center loop of the large coil (**figure 1, a**).

3 Continue forming a coil as illustrated in red in **figure 1**. Since the coil is large, you might find it easier to use your fingers to form the coil rather than pliers (**photo b**).

4 Form the rest of the wire shape using roundnose pliers, following the template from blue to yellow (**figure 1, b-c** and **photo c**).

5 The end of the wire is now crossing the outer ring of the coil. Trim the wire so it is about ¼ in. (6mm) past the point where it crosses the edge of the coil (**photo d**).

6 Grasp the end of the wire with roundnose pliers and make a small hook toward the coil. Slide the outside ring of the coil into the hook (**photo e**). Squeeze the hook closed using chainnose pliers.

Optional: Place the wire on an anvil or steel block and hammer it to add texture and harden the wire.

7 Open the loop (see "Basics," p. 3) on the earring finding and attach it to the wire shape at point **d** of **figure 1**. Close the loop.

8 Following **figure 2**, repeat steps 2-7 to make the second earring. – *Charlotte Miller*

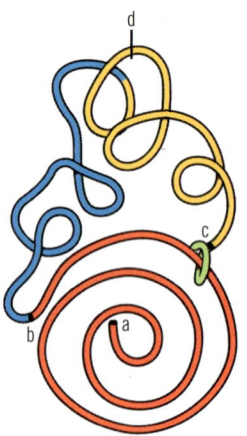

figure 1

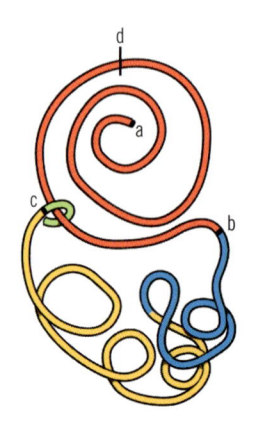

figure 2

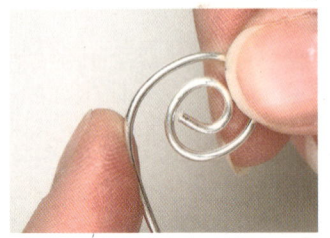

materials
- 32 in. (81cm) 14- or 16-gauge sterling silver wire, dead soft
- pair sterling silver earring findings with loops

Tools: roundnose and chainnose pliers, wire cutters, metal file
Optional: hammer, anvil or steel block